D1307593

ASK ABOUT ASIA

Mason Crest Publishers Inc.
370 Reed Road
Broomall, Pennsylvania 19008
(866) MCP-BOOK (toll free)

First printing

1 2 3 4 5 6 7 8 9 10

Library of Congress Cataloging-in-Publication Data on file at the Library of Congress.

ISBN 1-59084-201-4
ISBN 1-59084-198-0 (series)

Printed in Malaysia.

Adapted from original concept produced by
Vineyard Freepress Pty Ltd, Sydney.
Copyright © 1998 Vineyard Freepress Pty Ltd.

Project Editor	Valerie Hill
Text	Allen Roberts
Design	Denny Allnutt
Research	Peter Barker
Editor	Clare Booth
Cartography	Ray Sim
Consultant	Ishak Ismail
Cover Design	Vineyard Freepress
Images	Malaysia Tourism Promotion Board, Valerie Hill, Pavel German, Mike Langford, Ministry of Foreign Affairs (External Information Division) Malaysia, Australian War Memorial, Malaysian High Commission, Sentosa Development Corporation Singapore, Malaysian Industrial Development Authority (MIDA) Malaysia, Singapore Tourism Board, Ford Motor Co, Malaysian Airlines, Allen Roberts, Peter Barker.

COVER: Traditional Malay folk dance.

TITLE PAGE: Lanterns, Moon Cake Festival.

CONTENTS: *Perahu buatan barat*—wooden fishing boat, Kelantan.

INTRODUCTION: Boys on their way to a mosque.

Malaysia

MASON CREST PUBLISHERS

CONTENTS

MODERN MALAYSIA

DAILY LIFE

INTRODUCTION

MALAYSIA is a remarkable country. Remarkable because its people, from so many ethnic and cultural backgrounds, languages, and beliefs, chose democratically to become one nation. This federation has been so successful that today Malaysia is one of the most prosperous and stable countries in Southeast Asia.

This lush tropical land is still largely rural, with its mountains, rivers, and coasts inhabited by friendly, unhurried people who farm and fish as they have done for centuries. But now, after only 30 years, we see also the rapidly industrializing Malaysia, with its factories and multistory buildings. The challenge facing young Malaysians today is how to ensure that, with this progress, they do not neglect the family and national values that helped make their nation strong.

THE FEDERATION OF MALAYSIA

▲ The hibiscus is Malaysia's national flower.

▶ Sea stack in the Bako National Park.

▼ The mouse deer is only 9 in (23 cm) high.

Malaysia, like some other Southeast Asian countries, is made up of different land masses separated by sea. The Federation of Malaysia has two parts—West Malaysia and East Malaysia.

West Malaysia is a peninsula—reaching southward from the Asian continent to the thousands of islands of Southeast Asia. Heavy monsoon rain flows down its forest-covered mountains, feeding the thousands of creeks and rivers that enrich its fertile valleys and plains. The Main Range, which runs down the length of the peninsula, made land journeys so difficult in early times that most travel was along rivers or by sea. Today the peninsula has a network of roads.

East Malaysia is made up of two large states—Sabah and Sarawak. They occupy the northern part of the island of Borneo, which is separated from the peninsula by the South China Sea. The tiny oil-rich nation of Brunei is tucked between Sabah and Sarawak. The southern part of the island of Borneo is the state of Kalimantan, which is part of Indonesia.

◀ Butterflies with wings the size of a man's hand inhabit remote places.

CLIMATE

Malaysia, because it lies very close to the equator, has a humid hot-house climate with temperatures of up to 95°F. Rain can fall on 180 days in one year. The climate is gentler than those of many neighboring countries, because Malaysia is not affected by volcanoes, earth tremors, or the full force of monsoons and typhoons.

▲ The Cameron Highlands, at an altitude of 5,905 ft (1,800 m), are ideal for tea plantations.

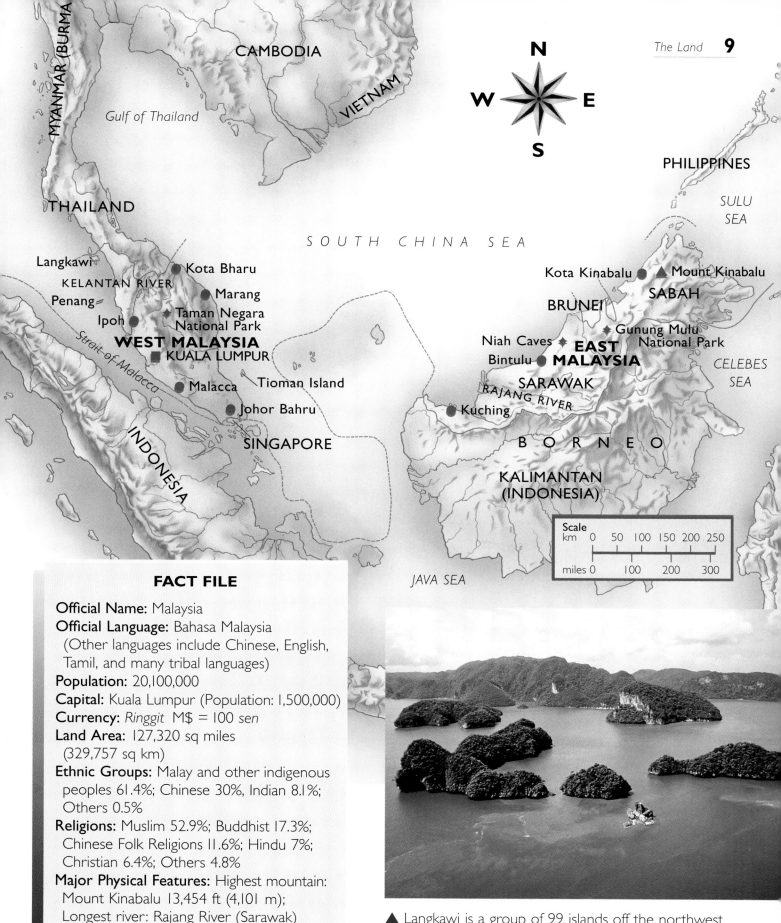

MYANMAR (BURMA)

CAMBODIA

VIETNAM

Gulf of Thailand

N
W E
S

PHILIPPINES

SULU
SEA

THAILAND

SOUTH CHINA SEA

Langkawi

KELANTAN RIVER
Penang
Ipoh

Kota Bharu

Marang

Taman Negara
National Park

WEST MALAYSIA

■ KUALA LUMPUR

● Malacca

● Johor Bahru

Tioman Island

SINGAPORE

INDONESIA

Strait of Malacca

Kota Kinabalu ● ▲ Mount Kinabalu

SABAH

BRUNEI

Niah Caves
Bintulu

Gunung Mulu
National Park

EAST
MALAYSIA

CELEBES
SEA

SARAWAK

RAJANG RIVER

● Kuching

B O R N E O

KALIMANTAN
(INDONESIA)

JAVA SEA

Scale
km 0   50 100 150 200 250

miles 0   100   200   300

FACT FILE

Official Name: Malaysia

Official Language: Bahasa Malaysia
(Other languages include Chinese, English,
Tamil, and many tribal languages)

Population: 20,100,000

Capital: Kuala Lumpur (Population: 1,500,000)

Currency: *Ringgit* M$ = 100 *sen*

Land Area: 127,320 sq miles
(329,757 sq km)

Ethnic Groups: Malay and other indigenous
peoples 61.4%; Chinese 30%, Indian 8.1%;
Others 0.5%

Religions: Muslim 52.9%; Buddhist 17.3%;
Chinese Folk Religions 11.6%; Hindu 7%;
Christian 6.4%; Others 4.8%

Major Physical Features: Highest mountain:
Mount Kinabalu 13,454 ft (4,101 m);
Longest river: Rajang River (Sarawak)
350 miles (560 km)

▲ Langkawi is a group of 99 islands off the northwest
coast of West Malaysia. Many have beautiful beaches
and clear waters rich in marine life.

GREEN FORESTS AND MUDDY RIVERS

Malaysia's heavy equatorial rainfall and very high humidity produce endless shades of green forest foliage. Most of the country has high temperatures, but up on the mountains the air is cool. You can see many different types of forest growing at different altitudes on Mount Kinabalu, Sabah, Malaysia's highest mountain, as you descend from its summit to sea level.

▲ Pitcher plants on Mount Kinabalu trap and digest insects to gain the nutrients missing from poor soil.

FORESTS ON MOUNT KINABALU

◄ The pinnacle of Mount Kinabalu is 13,454 feet (4,101 meters) above sea level—so high that snow sometimes falls on it. As we descend from its bare rocky summit, we enter a gloomy cloud forest. Here hot, damp air from below rises and condenses into mist at the cooler altitude. The forest is dwarfed, with stunted and gnarled trees no taller than a man. At about 9,800 ft (3,000 m) we see tree ferns and bamboo clumps, mosses and lichens covering taller trees. Animal life is sparse. Descending to 6,000 ft (1,800 m), we reach the foothills and the montane forest with taller trees up to 100 ft (33 m), and ferns and orchids.

◄ Tropical rainforest takes over at 3,000 ft (900 m), its soaring trees draped with ropey vines, lianas, ferns, and orchids. Little sunlight penetrates the thick leafy canopy high above. Myriads of unseen birds and animals call, and the pungent smell of decaying leaves fills the air.

◄ At sea level, palm trees grow in the salty beach sand. Here we find water-logged swamp forests, where mangrove roots trap black stinking river mud. These tidal areas are breeding and feeding grounds for bird and water life.

▲ Rainforest orchids grow, not in soil, but attached to the bark of trees.

▲ Orangutans inhabit Malaysia's rainforest.

Tropical monsoon rains flow down the steep forested mountains. This water descends through the thousands of muddy creeks and rivers that feed the country's fertile valleys and plains.

▲ Sungai Pandau waterfall, Pahang River in the peninsula of Malaysia.

▲ Tahan River in the peninsula of Malaysia. Neram trees form great arches over the fast-moving water, already heavy with mud.

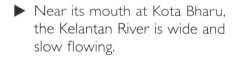

▶ Near its mouth at Kota Bharu, the Kelantan River is wide and slow flowing.

▲ Slash-and-burn, a method of clearing forest for small-scale cultivation.

▼ Clearing by machine for large-scale logging removes humus and topsoil. This results in soil erosion.

THE FRAGILE FOREST

Rainforests are made up of layers—the uppermost leaves of the tallest straight trees form a canopy, the roof of the forest; beneath the canopy, layers of lower trees, climbing vines, and smaller plants compete for space and light.

The floor of the forest is dark, and the earth is covered by a thin layer of humus formed by fallen leaves and trees, fruit, and dead animals. The soil in which rainforests grow is shallow, very sandy, and poor. It must have the cover of humus to enrich it and the canopy's umbrella of leaves to prevent it from being washed away by the torrents of tropical rain.

Under the shallow layer of topsoil is barren subsoil or rock. When the soil is washed away, no trees or other plants can live there. The forest dies.

▼ The rafflesia, more than 3 feet (1 meter) across, is the world's largest flower. Its smell of rotten flesh attracts insects, which pollinate it. After a few days, it darkens and withers away.

ORIGINAL PEOPLE

Nearly all of Malaysia's early history before the fifteenth century has been lost or destroyed. It is thought that the earliest inhabitants of the peninsula came south from Asia in ancient times. These people were short, dark skinned, and curly haired. They were one of several groups of first arrivals who lived by hunting and gathering. Over 4,000 years ago they were followed by immigrants from China, farmers who forced the earlier groups into the forests and hills, where a number still live today. The descendants of all these immigrants are known as *Orang Asli,* or "original people."

▼ Many of the "original people" were forest dwellers until the late twentieth century.

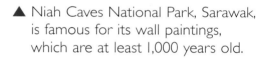
▲ Niah Caves National Park, Sarawak, is famous for its wall paintings, which are at least 1,000 years old.

EARLY RELIGION

Early jungle dwellers were animists who believed that every living thing has a soul or a spirit (known as *semangat*). They believed that these unseen beings had to be respected and worshiped in some manner to ensure that they did not cause harm to humans. For example, if a man saw or dreamed of an animal or bird that he believed was an evil omen, he would stop whatever he was doing until it was safe to proceed. Animist beliefs have been mixed with Malaysia's main religions.

▶ Masks, patterns, and decorations are all designed for a purpose—often as protection from evil spirits.

▲ Feathers from the sacred hornbill adorn
the headdress of this Iban man in Sarawak.

▶ The hornbill is Sarawak's state emblem.

Around 300 BC another migration from continental Asia
occurred—this time by a Malay people who came from Asia
by sea. They also colonized the Pacific as far as Hawaii and
westwards over the Indian Ocean almost to Africa. Today,
most of Malaysia's population is descended from all these
early migrations. Whether their ancestors were hunters
and gatherers, farmers or seafarers, they are all Malaysians.

▲ The custom of
stretching ear lobes
with heavy weights is
still practiced by a few
women in Sarawak.

▲ The Dongson drumsmiths of southern China and Vietnam have
left us a record of their early migration to Malaysia and other areas
of Southeast Asia. These artisans decorated bronze drums with
scenes from the world around them. Some depict warriors in
boats with drums near the stern. These decorations reveal much
about the possible ancestors of today's Malaysian people.

▶ Distinctive *batik* fabrics
have been worn in
Malaysia for centuries.

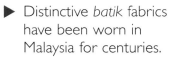

WHERE THE WINDS MEET...

The Malacca Strait, between the Malay Peninsula and Sumatra, has been since ancient times a safe anchorage for trading ships from many countries. Indian, Arab, and Chinese traders were coming there more than 1,500 years ago. By the fifteenth century, European traders had also become interested in Southeast Asia—because of its precious spices.

These European traders did not come by the overland Silk Road, used earlier to carry spices to Europe. They came by the sea route opened up by Portuguese navigators who rounded the Cape of Good Hope in the sixteenth century. They followed the monsoon winds to the Malacca Strait. There, protected from storms, they could anchor safely, repair their ships, and exchange cargoes. When the monsoon winds changed direction, and blew north, they would begin their homeward journey. For this reason, the Malacca Strait was known as "the place where the winds meet." For centuries, this haven for seafarers was also a meeting place for many nations—first Indians, then Arabs and Chinese, and later Portuguese, Dutch, and English.

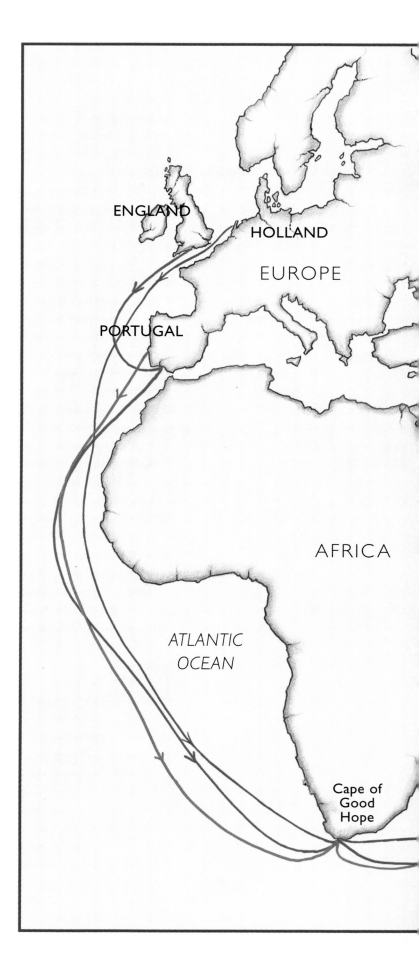

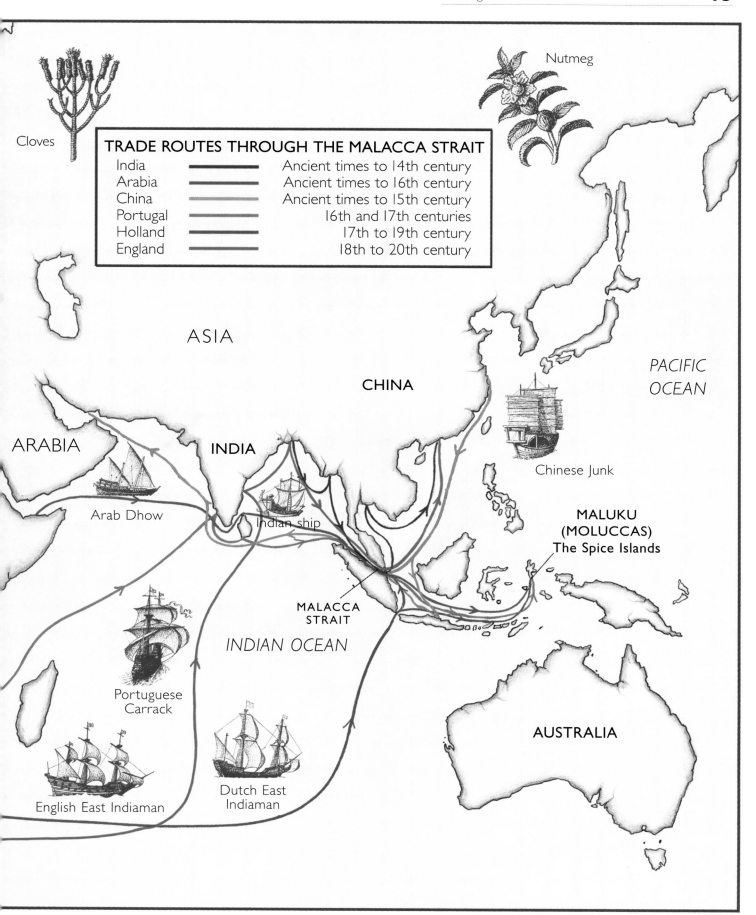

Cloves

Nutmeg

TRADE ROUTES THROUGH THE MALACCA STRAIT

India		Ancient times to 14th century
Arabia		Ancient times to 16th century
China		Ancient times to 15th century
Portugal		16th and 17th centuries
Holland		17th to 19th century
England		18th to 20th century

ASIA

CHINA

PACIFIC
OCEAN

ARABIA

INDIA

Arab Dhow

Indian ship

Chinese Junk

MALUKU
(MOLUCCAS)
The Spice Islands

MALACCA
STRAIT

INDIAN OCEAN

Portuguese
Carrack

AUSTRALIA

English East Indiaman

Dutch East
Indiaman

MANY PEOPLES

O ver the past 2,000 years the peoples who settled the peninsula and Borneo have absorbed a mixture of influences that have changed their lifestyles, languages, and beliefs. Most have come from countries that have traded with them. Indian merchants came for gold, aromatic woods, and spices, and trading centers sprang up along the shore. Some became powerful kingdoms ruled by Rajahs. India's former influence in Malaysia can still be seen in the ancient ruins of Hindu and Buddhist temples and in the hundreds of Indian Sanskrit words still spoken. Chinese merchants visited the Malays from ancient times to the fifteenth century. They traded in sandalwood, ivory, pearls, and edible birdnests. In the fifteenth century, the Chinese emperor gave sole trading rights with China to the Sumatran, Prince Paramesawara, who established and named Malacca.

▲ Indian ship.

▲ Indian influence is seen in Malay customs, court rituals, wedding ceremonies, food ingredients, *batik*, dances, and puppet plays. *Wayang kulit*, traditional Hindu shadow puppets, are cut out of leather and manipulated by rods. Only their shadows are seen on a screen. Behind the screen, a puppeteer uses many voices to tell long stories. A *gamelan* orchestra provides sound effects.

▶ Chinese junk.

◀ The elaborate embroidered dress of a Peranakan bride comes from China and her jeweled golden headdress from Malaya. Peranakans are both Chinese and Malayan. Their forebears were Chinese who came with trade ships to Malacca, then married Malayans and remained. Also known as Straits Chinese, many became wealthy. Their food, also a mixture of Chinese and Malayan, is known as *Nonya* (the word for "woman").

The most powerful influence upon the Malay way of life was a religious one. It came toward the end of the thirteenth century with traders from Arabia, the land of Mohammed. Paramesawara's son became a Muslim, and when he ascended the throne, he ordered everyone in his army to become Muslim. As a result, the Muslim faith (or Islam) spread quickly. Today most Malaysians are Muslims. Arabian and Muslim influence can be seen everywhere in Malaysia—the Jawa Script is the Malay language written in Arabic; there are mosques in every neighborhood. From their towers (or minarets), the long wailing sound of the call to prayer is heard everywhere in cities and villages throughout the country.

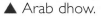

▲ Arab dhow.

▶ Mesjid Kampung Laut, a 300-year-old mosque near Malaysia's border with Thailand.

▲ Muslims celebrate the birthday of Mohammed.

THE RELIGION OF ISLAM

Islam was founded by Mohammed in the seventh century AD. Its teachings are found in a book called the *Koran*. These teachings are summarized in "The Five Pillars of Wisdom" in which a Muslim is required to:

1. confess his or her faith (make one's belief known publicly).
2. pray five times daily (first at dawn and finally after nightfall).
3. contribute money to help the poor.
4. fast during the month of Ramadan (food may not be eaten during daylight hours, only when it is dark).
5. make a pilgrimage to Mecca in Saudi Arabia at least once in a lifetime.

▶ Arabian Muslim head covering, a *tudung*, is still worn by many Malaysian women and girls.
◀ One of the head coverings worn by men and boys is the *songkok*.

EUROPEAN CONQUEST

By the end of the sixteenth century, European traders became interested in Malacca. In AD 1509 the Portuguese first visited the city, then in 1511 made three attacks on it. Two of these were unsuccessful because the shah's armed forces and fleets of merchants living there drove them off. But on their third attempt, the Portuguese blockaded the harbor and captured the city where they built a fortress (*A Famosa*). The next 130 years saw a power struggle between the Roman Catholic Portuguese and a number of Muslim empires in the region. Although the Portuguese used force to establish their control of trade, Malacca never regained its former glory. Their policies stirred up hatred, and they and their walled city came under continual attack.

▲ Portuguese carrack.

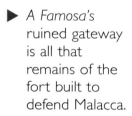

▶ *A Famosa's* ruined gateway is all that remains of the fort built to defend Malacca.

PORTUGUESE INFLUENCES

The Portuguese influence in Malaysia can still be seen in this folk dance, with its rapid hand and leg movements. Portuguese settlers were encouraged to marry Malay women. Their descendants in Malacca still speak a form of sixteenth-century Portuguese language.

◀ A statue in Malacca of Francis Xavier, pioneer Roman Catholic missionary to Southeast Asia, where he baptized about 30,000 people.

▶ Blessing of the ships at the Festival of St. Peter.

▲ Dutch East Indiaman.

In 1602, Dutch trading companies joined together to form the Dutch East India Company. Their plan was to set up their own trading empire and take control of the spice trade. They treated the Portuguese just as the Portuguese had treated the Malaccans more than a century earlier. The Dutch sailed up the Strait and blockaded the city. They then laid siege to *A Famosa* and after seven months captured the fortress, conquering the city in 1641. They went on to establish their monopoly of the spice trade, making their capital Batavia, now known as Jakarta, the capital of Indonesia.

◀ The Dutch ruled Malacca for 150 years. Their influence is seen mainly in architecture, as in this street with the *Studhuys* clock tower and Protestant Christ Church. These buildings look much like those of their homeland, Holland (The Netherlands).

PRECIOUS SPICES

Spices such as nutmeg and cloves have been used for centuries to flavor and preserve food. At first these highly prized and expensive cooking ingredients were grown only on the Moluccas (now Maluku), a group of islands east of Sulawesi. They were transported to the port of Malacca, and there reloaded onto ships for Europe and countries such as India and China.

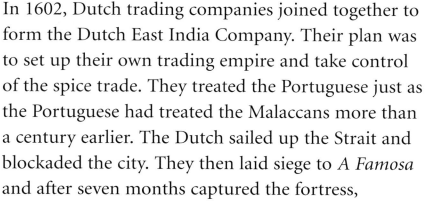

◀ Nutmeg.

Spicy foods are now popular all over the world. Malaysian food is known for flavors enhanced by different combinations of spices. A popular dish is *laksa*, a soup with noodles and portions of fish or meats or simply vegetables in a spicy curry and coconut milk broth.

◀ Cloves.

BRITISH RULE

From the sixteenth to the eighteenth century, England grew to become the world's leader in trade. The powerful East India Company had a monopoly over the export of tea from China to Europe. In 1795 Britain gained Malacca from the Dutch. The British had already established two other very important trading settlements along the Malacca Strait, Singapore and Penang.

▲ English East Indiaman.

These three "Straits Settlements" made Britain very successful in Southeast Asia. By the late nineteenth century, Britain had gained control of the peninsula and its strait and also Sarawak and Sabah, known as British North Borneo.

▶ Singapore became Britain's trading post in 1819. The Temenggong of Johor Riau, Malayan Sultan Hussein, heir to the throne of Singapore, sits between his son and British Sir Stamford Raffles to sign the agreement (Sentosa Island Museum).

▲ The British brought steam engines and built railway lines. For the first time it was possible to travel overland as well as by river. The grand Railway Station still in use in Kuala Lumpur has cupolas and minarets. Arched covered pavements give protection from the drenching tropical rain.

◀ ENGLISH LANGUAGE

During the British period a new social system was introduced and
- English became the main language spoken on the peninsula.
- Newspapers were published.
- Roman alphabets (as used in English) were used in written Malay, thus making it one of the few languages in the world written in two different scripts—Arabic and Roman.
- English literature—short stories, novels, and poetry—began to be read by Malayans.
- Malayans began to write their own literature and use it to depict the needs of ordinary people.
- A formal education system was introduced.

Tin mining in the peninsula created even greater wealth for Britain. Large numbers of Chinese were brought in as tin miners, and Indians as plantation workers. Serious conflict arose among Malay peninsula ruling families, and in Sabah a ten-year rebellion occurred because of new taxes. In spite of these problems, by the end of the nineteenth century, Britain was firmly in control of its colony, British Malaya.

▲ By the early 1900s, Singapore was Southeast Asia's major trading port. This display at the Sentosa Island museum recreates this bustling center with its people of many nationalities. These were exciting but dangerous times with pirates, secret societies, and power struggles.

▲ Rubber plantation.

▼ In the early 1900s when Henry Ford's cars rolled off America's new production lines, Malaya's rubber was used to make their tires. (1928 Model A Ford.)

RUBBER PLANTATIONS

When the demand for rubber became greater than supply, the British began to experiment with the cultivation of rubber trees. Seeds were carefully nurtured by Henry Ridley, director of the Singapore Botanic Gardens. He was so convinced that rubber plantations would make Malaya rich that he was called "Mad Ridley." He was proven to be right. By 1920 Malaya was growing half the world's rubber. Today it is the world's leading producer.

▶ Rubber is harvested by cutting (or tapping) a diagonal groove in the bark and collecting the sticky white latex that drips from it.

JAPANESE OCCUPATION

In 1941, during World War II, the Japanese invaded the Malayan peninsula. The British were prepared only for a sea attack on Singapore from the south and most of their guns were facing the sea. So when the Japanese landed in the north and came down the peninsula, the British were taken by surprise. Singapore's surrender gave the Japanese a control point for Southeast Asia and Australia.

▲ The quiet beaches of Kota Bharu where Japanese troops landed about two weeks before Christmas 1941. They quickly took control of the area.

▶ On bicycles, the Japanese moved rapidly down the peninsula, capturing Penang, Ipoh, Kuala Lumpur, and Johor Bahru, finally reaching Singapore, which they took within two months.

▲ The camouflaged skin of the flying lizard merges with a mossy branch. Soldiers learned that in jungle warfare, clothes mottled with green and brown merged into the green shadowy forest.

▶ A camouflaged soldier with leaves and ferns attached to his helmet could remain hidden just a few steps from his enemy (Sentosa Museum recreation).

JUNGLE WARFARE AND CAMOUFLAGE

In addition to the terrors of war, soldiers in Southeast Asia found the jungle a deadly enemy. In the incessant rain of the wet season, clothes rotted, and the ground became mud. Tropical diseases killed many. These conditions weakened both armies—the Japanese and the Allies (British, Australian, Chinese, Indian, Ghurkas, Malayans, and Eurasians).

In August 1945, the United States of America dropped two atomic bombs on Japan. Within a week Japan surrendered. Within the next month British forces had landed in Malaya. They found most of Singapore in ruins. Thousands were without food or shelter.

▲ Asian workers perch dangerously on top of a Japanese supply train crossing a 1,200 feet (366 m) long wooden bridge—part of the Burma Railway.

The Japanese built this rail link through 258 miles (415 kilometers) of some of the world's most rugged and disease-ridden jungle. To get their workforce, they carried off Malay, Javanese, Thai, and Burmese civilians along with British, Australian, American, and Dutch prisoners of war.

The railway was built in only 12 months. Of the 270,000 Asian civilian workers 240,000 did not return and have never been traced. About 30,000 prisoners of war died building the railway.

▲ The small chapel built at Changi prisoner of war camp in Singapore.

▼ After the war Japan gave to Singapore this memorial for people who died during the Japanese occupation.

INDEPENDENCE AND FEDERATION

After three and a half years of Japanese rule, the people of Malaya longed for self-government. They objected to the British plan for a Malay Union. In 1948 Britain helped set up the Federation of Malaya as a first step along the road to independence.

The communists wanted a socialist republic and formed guerrilla groups, who attacked British settlements and villages from jungle hideouts. A state of emergency was declared and only after seven years was it safe to hold an election. In 1957 the British flag was lowered and on 31 August the country gained its independence as the Federation of Malaya.

▲ Coins used in Malaya before Federation.

▼ Independence Memorial Hall, Malacca.

▲ National Monument in the Lake Gardens, Kuala Lumpur, commemorates those who fought and died for the country.

SINGAPORE

The important island port of Singapore was, for fifteen years, part of the Federation of Malaya, then briefly of the Federation of Malaysia. Later it withdrew and became an independent state.

▼ Raffles Hotel— an early postcard.

Singapore was originally founded in 1819 by colonial pioneer Sir Stamford Raffles. When he arrived there, it was only a small fishing village. He made it a free port for Britain (see page 20). From that time, it grew rapidly to become eventually one of the world's great trading centers, with ships from all over the world berthing at its docks.

▲ Merlion, a creature half mermaid and half lion, is the national symbol of Singapore. You can find this statue at the end of the waterfront promenade, Elizabeth Walk.

In 1963 the name was changed to the Federation of Malaysia and included Malaya, Singapore, North Borneo, and Sarawak. Brunei did not join. Indonesia and the Philippines did not agree with this union of states and confronted the newly formed Federation. Fighting continued until 1965. But this did not prevent the inauguration of the Federation of Malaysia in 1963, with Tunku Abdul Rahman as its first prime minister.

▶ Independence is celebrated each year on 31 August, *Merdeka* (Freedom) Day.

◀ Malaysia's flag has red and white stripes to represent its federated states and the crescent and star to show its Muslim state religion.

MALAYSIA'S NATIONAL ANTHEM

My country, my native land,
The people living united and progressive,
May God bestow blessing and happiness,
May our ruler have a successful reign.

▲ Malaysian coins in use after Federation.

After 1963, our country was no longer Malaya, but MALAYSIA.

▶ The people of Malaysia, although they have come from many different countries and have widely differing backgrounds and beliefs, are united as one nation.

GOVERNMENT

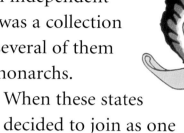

Malaysia is a constitutional monarchy. Before it became an independent nation, it was a collection of states, several of them ruled by monarchs.

When these states decided to join as one federated nation, they had to choose a form of government that would best represent them. After consultation with Great Britain, a draft constitution was accepted. It was similar in many ways to the Westminster system of Great Britain and its Commonwealth countries. This kind of government has been stable and effective in Malaysia for many years.

▲ Parliament House, Kuala Lumpur.

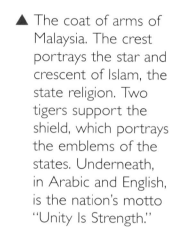

▲ The coat of arms of Malaysia. The crest portrays the star and crescent of Islam, the state religion. Two tigers support the shield, which portrays the emblems of the states. Underneath, in Arabic and English, is the nation's motto "Unity Is Strength."

▼ The Malaysian currency note is the *Ringgit* (M$) or Malaysian dollar, which is divided into 100 cents (*sen*).

◀ Prime Minister, Dr. Mahathir Mohamad. The Malaysian Parliament, as in Great Britain, has a Prime Minister. It has two chambers: the House of Representatives, where parliamentarians elected by the people make the nation's laws; and the Senate, which reviews laws before they can be passed.

▶ The National Mosque represents the close connection between the government of Malaysia and the state religion, Islam.

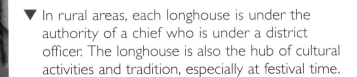

▼ In rural areas, each longhouse is under the authority of a chief who is under a district officer. The longhouse is also the hub of cultural activities and tradition, especially at festival time.

▲ As in Britain's Westminster system, the powers of Malaysia's monarchy are limited by the constitution. However, unlike the queen or king of Great Britain, who reigns for a lifetime, the nine rulers of Malaysia reign in turn, each for five years.

CULTURES OF MANY PEOPLES

The Ministry of Culture, Arts, and Tourism seeks to preserve the identity of ethnic groups. While this government policy is based mainly on Malay traditions, the Ministry also supports cultural expression of all other ethnic groups, so long as they remain within the law.

▲ The traditional costume of the Tagar Murut people is decorated with beadwork. Beads are stitched onto the hat.

▶ Traditional items like floor coverings and baskets are woven from natural materials including dried bark, grasses, and leaves.

▲ Weaving *songket*, or brocade, of silk, gold, and silver threads, formerly worn only by royalty. It is now used for many purposes—handbags, wall hangings, and clothes for special occasions, such as weddings. *Songket* workshops are found mainly near Kota Bharu, Kelantan.

MALAYSIA AND THE WORLD

▲ Packaged goods ready for transport.

Malaysia's influence extends far beyond its own borders. It belongs to ASEAN (Association of Southeast Asian Nations), in which the member nations plan ways to improve their economies, trade among themselves and with other nations, and also protect their environments. Malaysia has been increasingly involved in world affairs since becoming a more industrialized nation. This is seen in its numerous conferences with various international leaders, its place in world tourism, and its hosting of such international events as the 1998 Commonwealth Games.

▲ Orchids are among the most beautiful exports and are favored for wedding bouquets.

▶ Officer of the armed forces, which maintain law and order, provide defense, and assist in international peace-keeping.

◀ The birdlike *wau* or moon
▶ kite, which is so much a part of Malaysian culture, flies around the world as the emblem of Malaysia Airlines.

▼ Many tourists come from Scandinavian countries and Germany. Backpackers, conference and tour groups, and others can stay in resorts or homes.

▲ The prime minister meets with leaders of other nations. He often officiates at conferences such as ASEAN and APEC (Asia Pacific Economic Cooperation) to improve the free flow of trade in the region.

▼ Children wearing their traditional dress perform on International Children's Day.

▶ Sports fishermen come to Sabah from April to October when marlin can be caught offshore.

HARVESTING LAND AND SEA

Malaysia, although not a large country, is rich in natural resources, which help it feed its population of more than 20 million people. A tropical climate, rich soils, and abundant water supply guarantee good crops. They include fruits such as bananas (40 varieties), mangoes, papaya (pawpaw), pineapples, watermelons, and guavas. At higher altitudes, citrus fruits, such as mandarins, thrive. Abundant vegetables are grown and sold in local markets.

▲ Malaysia's climate guarantees a constant supply of fresh vegetables.

▶ Red (sweet) peppers laid out to dry in the sun. This vegetable is used in many dishes.

▼ Cocoa pods are sorted and hulled. The beans are highly nutritious and are used to make cocoa and chocolate.

▶ Breadfruit is used to make a kind of flour, which when baked tastes like wheat bread.

▲ Peanuts are delicious to eat raw or crushed in *satay* sauce. A major crop, its oil is used in cooking and also in machine oil and paints.

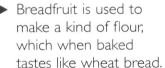

▶ Harvesting pepper, a pungent spice. The seeds are dried in the sun and sold as peppercorns or as a powder.

Huge amounts of rice, Malaysia's staple diet, are grown in paddy fields. Fishing, an important source of local food, needs to be increased to meet the needs of Malaysia's growing population. Major crops supply secondary industry—Malaysia is the world's largest rubber producer (see page 20), and hardwood timber is a major primary industry (see page 32).

▲ Rice seedlings grow under water.

▲ Ripe grain is mechanically harvested.

▲ Harvested rice must be kept dry to prevent mold from forming in Malaysia's humid climate.

▲ Lobsters for dinner tonight!

▶ These fresh fish will be cooked and served in a variety of dishes.

▼ Drying *ikan bilis*, small but strong-flavored fish served with many meals.

▶ Cattle, which are highly valued, are not kept in large numbers.

INDUSTRY

Malaysia in recent years has developed strong secondary industries to process its natural resources. Factories treat and bail its rubber and mill its timber, while oil and natural gas from offshore rigs are now processed in its refineries. There are also factories making petroleum-based products and fertilizers. From the early 1970s, enormous growth has occurred in the manufacture of electronic equipment—radios, tape recorders, stereo equipment, microwave ovens, air conditioners, and computer hardware. Malaysia is one of the world's leaders in the manufacture of electronic semiconductors.

▲ Fabrication of wafers used to make silicon chips for computers.

▲ Liquid natural gas (LNG) plant in Bintulu, Sarawak, is now the largest exporter of LNG in the world.

▼ Hardwood logs felled in Malaysian forests were once floated downstream for milling. Most of Malaysia's timber is made into furniture, veneer, plywoods, and particle board. Because of heavy tree felling, there is concern that ancient forests will be destroyed.

▲ Oil rig off the coast of Sarawak.

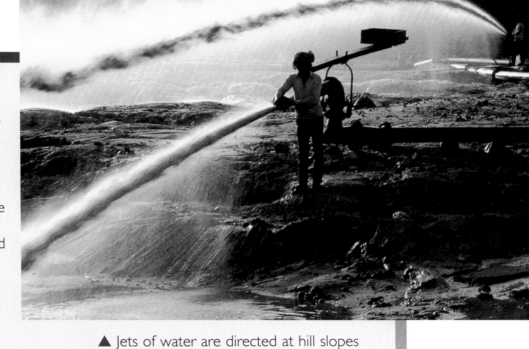

TIN AND PEWTER

For many years Malaysia has supplied most of the world's tin. More than one thousand years ago tin was being mined in the region. During the nineteenth and twentieth centuries, the British mined and exported large amounts to make decorative or useful kitchen and tableware and containers for food and other commodities. Today tin is also used to make solder and metal alloys for industry.

◀ Tin is the main metal in high quality pewter goods exported worldwide. This assembly-line worker uses a lathe to make pewterware.

▲ Jets of water are directed at hill slopes to loosen tin-bearing soil for pumps.

▶ Multimillion *ringgit* tin dredge used for removing tin-rich ore for treatment.

▼ Plantations of palm oil trees yield vegetable oil used in margarine and many other foods. It is rich in vitamins E and A.

▲ Palm oil fruits are delivered to processing factories.

▶ Quality control of palm oil products.

KUALA LUMPUR—K.L.

Kuala Lumpur is the federal capital of Malaysia. Its name means "muddy river mouth," which describes the place where it began as a ramshackle tin-mining settlement in the mid 1800s. Today, it is a bustling modern city of one and a half million people with skyscrapers of concrete, steel, and glass, six-lane highways, and highly developed technology.

▲ Tin mines similar to this one have been operating in Malaysia for 150 years.

▼ Deer Park is part of Taman Tasek Perdana, the capital's largest park, which also contains an aviary and orchid garden.

► Latest-model cars move quickly on Kuala Lumpur's freeways.

Kuala Lumpur's transformation began in the late 1800s when the British Resident, Frank Swettenham, made it the country's administration center. He encouraged local businessmen to pull down the settlement's old wooden huts and replace them with British colonial-style buildings. Today, you can still see many of these, along with other nineteenth century buildings such as temples and mosques.

◀ Petronas Towers with their minaret-shaped spires, currently the world's tallest buildings at 1,873 ft (571 m).

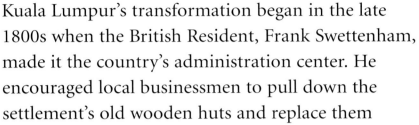

▲ Chinese opera and Indian food reveal the city's varied
▼ cultural background.

▲ Nineteenth-century Abdul Samad Building against a twentieth-century skyline.

◀ After a hot day, people flock to the night market, or *pasar malam*, to shop and socialize in the cool of the evening.

OLD AND NEW

Malaysia is a rapidly changing nation—a land of contrasts, where old and new ways continue side by side. When a new skyscraper is opened, it is not unusual to see Buddhist priests chanting or Muslims reading an ancient blessing. Cars and trucks roar past villages of thatch-roofed cottages where buffaloes still plough paddy fields. Educational opportunities for children in villages enable them to take their place in business and government. Many young people from farming and fishing communities are employed in cities as doctors, computer programmers, or factory workers. The Prime Minister and government want Malaysia to be a strong and prosperous modern nation. But they do not want its people to forget traditions of the past—especially the simple but important ones about caring for families and respecting others.

▲ The coffin of a dead chief in Kuching was raised toward heaven on huge intricately carved poles.

▲ A satellite dish focuses on the sky as part of a world communications network.

▲ Early wooden steps were cut from logs.
▶ Multistory buildings have steel escalators.

◀ Iban women change into glittering silver costumes for celebrations in their villages or for international events.

◀ Paved roads and high earnings mean that more people are buying cars.

▼ Modern roads cut through ancient forests.

◀ Indian bullock carts once lumbered along in traffic, but today they are no longer permitted on Malaysia's busy roads, except as tourist attractions in Malacca.

BATIK

Hand crafted *batik* fabrics are printed and dyed by wax resist methods known in ancient Egypt and Sumeria.

▶ Repeat patterns stamped in hot wax remain uncolored when fabric is dyed.

▼ In free form patterns the design is drawn with wax.

◀ Iban men in traditional dress demonstrate how, in earlier times, rivers were navigated

▼ . . .while these tourists, wearing protective life jackets and helmets, prepare to shoot the rapids in a fast-flowing river.

▲ This Iban family lives in a longhouse community.

FAMILIES AND KAMPUNG

Malaysians for thousands of years have been village people and every village (*kampung*) a collection of closely connected families. In recent times the *kampung* has become larger and more developed, with facilities such as electricity and libraries, but family lifestyles and traditions continue.

Extended families include parents and children, and often grandparents and grandchildren. Life is often crowded and lacking in privacy, but no one seems to mind, for Malaysians value their family life and its traditions above all else.

"Selamat pagi!" a friendly morning greeting to passersby.

EXTENDED FAMILY

Although the father is responsible for earning money for his family, many women also work—sometimes in markets, family businesses, or plantations. The mother often manages both the home and the family business.

Both city and *kampung* families appreciate having a sister, aunt, or grandmother to watch over children while parents work. Families dress up and attend festivals together; and children are included in family activities such as weaving, or selling fish in a beach-side market.

◀ Brothers, cousins, and friends play sports together.

▲

Although there have been many changes, children still respect their parents. Each year in a Muslim ceremony (*Hari Raya Puasa*) children take their father's hand and ask his blessing and forgiveness for any disobedience to him.

▶ *Kampung* friends live close by.

▼ Like Indian royalty, a Malay groom and bride sit enthroned on a dais in their wedding finery. A wedding guest pays her respects.

FAMILY HOMES

In cities, brick and plaster houses of early European design are often kept cool by closing shutters during the heat of the day. Housing estates for employees are being built near workplaces. Air-conditioning is used extensively in new city buildings.

▶ You can fish from the veranda in a traditional wooden house over water, high on stilts. Rural houses, near rice fields and fruit trees, are also raised so cool air can flow underneath and through open windows.

A RICH MIX OF FOOD

Because Malaysia is made up of people from so many different countries, its food is extremely varied, a mix of sweet, sour, hot, and bitter flavors. Malay food is usually served

with rice, the country's staple food. Chicken, fish, and prawns, and sometimes beef, lamb, and goat are served. Pork is forbidden (*haran*) within Islam. Malay food uses a wide range of spices, often in sauces ranging from hot with chili to cool with milky coconut. Some of the delicious foods available are traditional Chinese, *Nonya*, a blend of Chinese and Malay, and Southern Indian, with its curries and spices.

▲ Chinese roasted ducks hang on hooks in a roadside market.

▶ Bringing home fresh produce.

▼ A family sorting fish for sale in the local market.

▶ Making *roti*, a flat circular bread eaten with Indian meals.

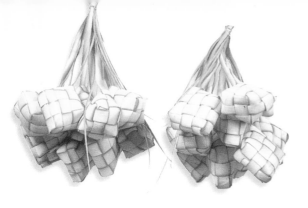

▲ *Ketupat*, cooked bundles of rice wrapped in young banana leaves, are eaten with *satay*.

▼ Open-air stall, with *satay* and other delicacies, in Kota Bharu.

FOOD AT YOUR FINGERTIPS

Open-air stalls sell favorite foods, such as *satay* (spicy grilled meat on skewers), *pisang goreng* (fried battered bananas), and *laksa* (coconut and chili soup over meats, vegetables, and seafoods). Vendors often cook food along roadsides, where passersby can stop for a snack. Others push trollies through the suburbs and bring favorite dishes to your door.

▲ Sweets vendor. A favorite dessert is the spectacular iced *kacang*—a mixture of ice shavings, chunks of *agar agar* (a seaweed jelly), sweet potato, and beans, topped with colored syrups and condensed milk.

◀ The prickly durian fruit has a bad smell, but delicious creamy flesh.

▶ The family custom of gathering together to eat is one of Malaysia's most valued traditions. This family begins a meal by cleansing the fingers of the right hand, which is used to eat food.

▲ The yellow school bus is as common in Malaysia as in America.

SCHOOL DAYS

Malaysia, a nation of fast-growing industry, business, and high technology, needs a sound education system. To ensure this, the government has introduced national curricula and examinations. Children begin classes at around six years of age and complete 11 years of schooling—six primary and five secondary. Secondary school prepares them for technical and vocational work. Those who seek a university education must first complete two further years and gain a higher school certificate. Some of the many residential schools provide special classes linked with universities. There are also more than 150 school hostels that enable pupils from rural areas to attend primary and secondary schools in major towns.

▲ Students march in a National Day parade, 31 August.

◄ ▲ Playground and classroom in a state primary school for boys and girls. Boys wear shorts and white shirts. Girls have long skirts and head coverings.

◄ Parents assist in
► schools—serving cooked lunches in Kelantan, and accompanying a school excursion in the Cameron Highlands.

LANGUAGES

The national language is Bahasa Malaysia, which is taught in every school. But because of the many different ethnic communities, there is a People's Own Language (POL) scheme to ensure that all children have opportunity to learn to read and write their own languages.

▶ Arabic is taught in this Muslim school for teenage boys. They learn to read the *Koran* in Arabic. These students are school boarders and wear the traditional robe (*jubah*).

Special classes in state schools provide lessons for pupils to learn languages other than their own. English is compulsory for all children from the time they start school at six years of age. Students must attain a high level of English before they can enter a university.

◀ In addition to Bahasa Malaysia and English, Mandarin Chinese is taught at the many Chinese schools. These three languages lay a foundation for business or international careers.

▶ Two of the 3,000 Chinese characters students must know to write Chinese.

▶ Education also takes place outside formal schooling. A father carefully teaches his son that Muslims wash their feet before entering the mosque, their holy place.

▶ When his father arrives back from fishing, this small boy from Kota Bharu boards his boat. Later he will help clean and market the fish. Once he would have followed his father and become a fisherman— now his schooling will enable him to choose from many careers.

VISITING MALAYSIA

When you visit Malaysia, plan to savor the country's great variety. It is easy to get around, as most people speak English and are very friendly. You can go to out-of-the way places to enjoy nature in the forests, in peaceful farming or fishing *kampungs* or on different islands. Or you can find excitement in bustling cities with their local and international entertainment, restaurants, and shops. Malaysia, like its food, has something for every taste.

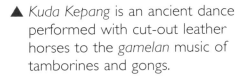

▲ *Kuda Kepang* is an ancient dance performed with cut-out leather horses to the *gamelan* music of tamborines and gongs.

WHEN YOU VISIT

Malaysians will be delighted when you, as a visitor, respect their customs.

DO
- Use only your right hand when shaking hands and receiving objects.
- Use your right-hand fingers for eating.
- Remove your shoes and leave them at the door when entering a Malay house, a mosque, or a Hindu temple.
- Wear respectable clothing when you visit a Malaysian family.

DO NOT
- Touch the head of a Malaysian person.
- Shake hands with a female if you are male—just nod your head and smile.
- Point at someone with your index finger or gesture with a foot.
- Put your feet on a table.
- Take a dog, pork or alcohol into a Malaysian home.

◀ ▲
Climb Mount Kinabalu in Sabah, or ford a river in Taman Negara National Park.

▼ Explore the largest cave chamber in the world, the Deer Cave, in Gunung Mulu National Park, Sarawak. It is large enough inside to park 200 double-decker buses.

◄ See baby green turtles hatch and scramble for the water. Plan ahead to watch the giant leatherback turtles come ashore south of Marang to lay their eggs in beach sands.

▼ Enjoy traditional dance performances

▲ . . .don't tread on a stone fish, which has poisonous spines and lurks in the shallows of ocean reefs

▼ . . .wander along the aisles of Kelantan's huge food market.

▲ Spinning tops, or *gasing*, are streamlined works of art. They can be as big as dinner plates and weigh up to 12 lbs (5.5 kg). Master spinners with skill and strength can set a top spinning for two hours.

INDEX

N

National Anthem 25
National Monument 24
national parks 8, 9, 12, 44
Nonya 16, 40
nutmeg 19

O

oil 32
original people 12, 13, 25, 27, 29, 36, 37, 38

P

palm oil 33
Paramesawara 16, 17
parliament 26
Penang 9, 20, 22
peninsula 8, 14, 20, 21, 22
Peranakan 16
Petronas Towers 35
pewter 33
plantations 21, 33
plants 8, 10, 11, 22, 28
population 9, 30
Portuguese 14, 18, 19
prime minister 25, 26, 29, 36
puppets 16

R

Raffles, Sir Stamford 20, 24
Rahman, Tunku Abdul 25
rainforests 10, 11
religion 9, 12, 16, 17, 18, 19, 23, 25, 26, 36, 39
reptiles 22, 45
rice 31, 40, 41
ringgit 9, 26, 33
rivers 8, 9, 11
rubber 21, 30, 31, 32

S

Sabah 8, 9, 10, 20, 21, 27
Sarawak 8, 9, 12, 13, 20, 32, 44
schools 42, 43
ships 14, 15, 16, 18, 19, 20, 24
Singapore 20, 21, 22, 23, 24, 25
South East Asia 7, 8, 13, 14, 18, 20, 21, 22, 28
spice 14, 15, 16, 18, 19, 30, 40
spinning tops 45
sport 28, 29, 37, 39
statues 24
Strait of Malacca 9, 14
Straits Chinese 16, 40

T

tea 8
technology 32, 33, 34, 36, 42
temples 16
timber 31, 32
tin 21, 22, 33, 34
tourism 27, 28, 29, 37, 44, 45
trade 14, 15, 16, 18, 19, 20, 24, 28, 32, 33
transport 21, 22, 23, 34, 36, 37, 40, 41, 42

V

villages 17, 24, 36, 38, 39

W

wayang kulit 16
weaving 27, 38
West Malaysia 8, 9
Westminster system 26, 27
winds 14
World War II 22, 23, 24
writing 17, 20, 43